THE
GOLDEN BOOK
OF

CREATING, MARKETING & SELLING BOOKS

UNLOCKING THE SECRET OF SUCCESS

FREE & INEXPENSIVE WAYS TO CREATE, PROMOTE AND SELL YOUR BOOKS

BY TIFFANY KAMENI

PRACTICAL KNOWLEDGE FOR FIRST TIME AUTHORS

THE GOLDEN

BOOK OF SELLING

AND

MARKETING BOOKS

e-book.

Individual results vary. Author, Tiffany Kameni, is not responsible or liable for any individual results. By purchasing this e-book, buyer acknowledges that he or she understands that this book is solely for educational purposes only. Buyer is responsible for his or her own individual results as an Author.

Note From the Author

Dear Reader,

As a first-time author, you will face the hardships of trying to sell your books (unless you're famous, of course). You don't have the luxury of a dedicated audience, and you don't have the big bucks to shell out to publish or market your book. What should you do?

The Golden Book of Marketing and Selling Books is a non-traditional, unconventional read that will show you how to get around spending thousands of dollars! In this book, you will learn how to improvise and make the best out of what you do have!

This book is also great for authors who have published one or two books previously, but haven't had success in selling those books. The Golden Book of Marketing and Selling Books is an information-filled read that will teach you how to do much of the work yourself!

Best wishes,

Tiffany Buckner-Kameni

Table of Contents

Introduction

You have written your book, and now you are ready to publish it, but with so many authors out who never sell a book or any more than ten books; how do you avoid becoming just another author?

Fact is, there are many mistakes made by unseasoned authors. It's simply because they don't know what to do, where to go, and many times; their funds are limited. The average person doesn't become an average author until they have published at least three or more books. This isn't great news for the many that have invested so much time and money into their projects, only to find themselves marketing amiss.

If you are like me, you wanted to find a nice e-book or book to tell you what to do, but 200 pages of foreign words and thousands of links can be discouraging and overwhelming. When you have written your book and are ready to publish, you want step-by-step instructions of what to do, how to do it, where to go and what to expect. You want to know what works and what does not work.

That's why I created this step-by-step guide to help you get published and do it right the first time. This guide won't give you tons of useless information and links that take you into confusing discussions that you have to dig your way through. Who wants to go through a bunch of bones trying to get to the meat?

In this guide, you will not only learn how and where to market your e-books, but you will learn how to save yourself hundreds, if not thousands of dollars by learning to do most of the work yourself. You will avoid many of the blocks in the road that trip a lot of first-time writers.

E-book Versus Print

When you're a first time author, you should always explore e-books first; all the same, there is nothing like the feel of your own book between your fingers. There are some facts that you may want to consider before you make your decision as to whether or not you want to print your book or simply keep it digital.

Printed books are awesome when you are willing to go out and market them. Most people think that they'll be able to sell the bulk of their print from the comfort of their own homes, but the reality is that while you may be able to sell some books online, the majority of your audience is outside when you are an unknown author. Therefore, print books are a great way to go if you don't mind burning the gas and investing the time needed.

With print books you need physical copies. There are many websites and companies that specialize in printing books, but they usually charge the customer higher rates than other printers. In addition, the author doesn't earn much on royalties if they sell their books at the price they want to sell them for. Consequentially, the author has to sell their books at higher rates just to make a profit. This could discourage potential buyers, especially if they don't know you or your work. In addition, you may become discouraged by the lack of sells. Remember this: Many well-known authors don't charge excessive rates for their books because they expect their books to sell in volumes, and this encourages buys; but if you are an unknown selling a book with the same type of information for more, you will lose sells.

When you go out, you should have at least 50-100 copies of your book ready to sell and already signed. (Get a signature stamp; it'll save you time.) If you're having to pay ten dollars per copy of your own book from the printer, you're already at a loss because you'll have to charge at least fifteen to twenty-five dollars just to earn a profit. This is okay if your book is more than 150 pages, but if you have a small book (less than 100 pages), people won't be too eager to pay what you are requesting. It is better to buy it low and sell it low. We'll discuss how later in this book.

E-books are the in-thing right now because they eliminate the wait that print books require to arrive in the mail, and they are less expensive than prints. With today's technology, readers can simply download the electronic books to their computers, cellphones, IPADs, Kindles or whatever mobile devices they are using and read them immediately.

Contrary to popular belief, you will still have to get out and physically market your e-books because there are quite a few authors in today's market that are selling the same knowledge that you are selling. When a customer is trying to make a decision, they will usually take the price, look, and preview of your book under consideration. When you are face-to-face with a customer, you don't have a competitor standing nearby offering a better deal or a better product. While you may get quite a bit of sells from your online audience, personal sells will serve as a huge benefit to your book because people love to support local authors. Social networking sites may bring in sells, but don't put too much of your faith into online sells until you've conquered the offline market.

As a first-time author, it is always great to publish your book as an electronic copy as well as a printed copy, but if you can't afford to do both, go for an electronic copy first to test the market. See what works and does work before you begin investing money into the project.

Getting Started With

Your Book

Hopefully, you have already begun to write the book and you already have the title for it, but if you don't, you can still learn from this manuscript. Here are a few tips to help you get started.

    1. The name of your book should not be the first thing you jot down. Sure, you've thought for hours and you've come up with this very catchy name that you insist on using, but if you prematurely name the book, you will have to make sure

your book's subject matter does not bleed outside of the book's title. For example, let's say that you wrote a book about how to deal with interfering ex spouses. You name the book <u>The Ex-Terminator</u>. As you begin your writing journey, you get this brilliant idea to incorporate advice on how to overcome the pressures of being a step parent and how to love and be loved by your step children. Now, your great idea for the title doesn't fit the subject matter anymore. So, you change it to <u>Step to Step-Riddle of the Ex-Terminator</u>. All of a sudden, you find yourself advising the readers on how to have a happy and healthy marriage with someone who's divorced, and now; you're having to change the name again.

Oftentimes, writers love the first title that they chose, so when the book's content bleeds outside of the name, they simply keep adding to it just to keep the name and cover the book's content. They begin to think from within the limited confines of the name that they initially chose for their book. It is always better to come up with the name after you have completed the book and not before. This way, you can better choose a name that is fitting and speaks to the subject matter of the entire book, without being extra wordy.

2. Table of contents are great to begin with. When writing a book, it's

sometimes hard to come up with the chapters, especially if you're coming up with them as you go along. Some people may like coming up with the chapters as they write, but I have found that the easiest way to come up with content for your book is to write the chapters down, or better yet, type them in your document. How does this help? Knowing what you are writing about helps you to flow right into the subject matter. As you go along, you will more than likely get ideas for new chapters and content, but it's easy to insert the new information and just flow from there. Let's say you are writing a book about raising Siberian Huskies. Your table of content may look like:

...Introduction

....Introduction to the Siberian Husky

....Breed Information

....Behaviors

....Why a Husky Isn't For Everyone

....Exercise and Routine

....Common Health Problems

....The Misbehaved Husky

....The Great Escape Artist- Husky Ran Away...Again!

....Is a Husky Right For Me

You start writing and find that in your chapter *'The Misbehaved Husky,'* you wrote about one of their personality flaws, and that flaw is that Huskies love to escape. You go on to share your experiences with the readers about your husky and how you lured him back into the car after a three-mile chase. That's an exceptional improvement from the usual five-mile chase that he used to take you on. Because of this, you now have to delete the suggested chapter, *'The Great Escape Artist-Husky Ran Away...Again!'* You did; however, get an idea about fencing and gadgets that are great for keeping them from scaling the walls, so you decide to add, *'Husky Proofing Your Life'* into the table of contents. You will find that as you start each chapter, it will be easier to fill in the content with a prepopulated table of contents rather than a blank slate. In addition, you may get ideas for new chapters as you flow into your book.

3. Keep your content relevant. As a writer, you may continually get ideas as you write, but sometimes, the ideas aren't relevant to the book or the book's title. For example, you may find yourself going from writing a how-to book about fishing to writing about great-tasting fish recipes. Someone reading this book may find that you're all over the place and abandon reading your book. When your mind races off into new ideas, open up a second document and insert the new

information as a chapter for your next book. If people really enjoy your how-to guide, they'll more than likely come back for more of your books.

Author Eagerness

Syndrome

Before you go running to your doctor, this is not
an actual ailment; it's just a way of thinking.

Author Eagerness Syndrome (by my
interpretation) is an author who is so anxious to
get their books out that they skip over some of
the vital steps.

I've been there. My first book was the perfect
example. One night, I began writing what I
thought was going to be an article, but the page
count kept growing and growing, and suddenly

I realized that I was writing a book. I was excited and determined to finish immediately, so I wrote that book in one night and published it the next day. As a result, my book's content, formatting, and cover design were hideous.

You may be saying that you're not anxious, but you are eager to get your book finished and published. If so, you're obviously anxious, and the closer you get to the finished line, the more anxious and careless you will become with your book's content. If this is your first book, this way of thinking is absolutely normal because you're only excited about the prospect of being an author. This is a great accomplishment for anyone. At the same time, this is why most first-time authors crash and burn with their first submission.

Overly anxious authors usually skip over editing, formatting, professional cover designs, web sites, professional author bios, professional book synopses, press kits, professional photos and so on. I thought the same way when I published my first book. I thought about that nice photo that I took of myself in the living room and decided that it would suffice. I decided to do my own cover design (before I was a professional graphic designer), and I thought my grade A English didn't need editing. After I published my book and it began to sell, I went back and reread it again and again. I was so humiliated by what I read. I had errors going throughout that book, and it wasn't formatted the right way.

What you may not realize is that your book needs 100% professionalism. If you hold back, your sells will pay the price.

What are the symptoms of being overly anxious?

- 〉 Trying to hurry up and finish the book.
- 〉 Trying to rush up a name for the book.
- 〉 Trying to publish the book without getting <u>professional</u> help or refusing to wait for the funds to come in for <u>professional</u> help.
- 〉 Ignoring the fact that you need an ISBN and barcode.
- 〉 Getting angry at people for not buying

your book and vowing not to ever support them in their endeavors. How dare they not support your dream of spending two dollars and earning 2 million in return!

⟩ Deleting paragraphs in your book because they are taking the book in a different direction, and you don't want to invest the time researching and adding these new branches to the book.

⟩ Feeling anxious when you see another author has published their book. *(They didn't wait on you? The nerve!)*

⟩ Asking others to write a chapter for your book to fill in the pages so you can hurry up and publish the book. You've made it to 60 pages, but you wanted 100. Now, you're chasing down 40 people and asking them to submit an article. (By the way, there is nothing wrong with getting others to submit an article; it's just that it shouldn't be done to pacify eagerness).

In short, AES is simple desperation.

Now, you need an antidote and it's simple:

1. Make a list of everything that needs to be done before you start your book. If you have already started the book, take a moment and make this list. Your list should look like:

Name	Pricing Info	Phone
Insert Editor's Name	Insert	Editor's

Here	Editor's Price Here	Contact Number
Insert Cover Designer's Name Here	Insert CD's Price	Cover Designer's Contact Number

2. Find the people you need at the prices you can afford, but look for professionalism. Look at their portfolios, read the customer reviews and don't settle for the first person that you come across. Ask other authors about the people and companies that they've used as well as their experience with them.

3. Start a savings account with your local bank or get a prepaid banking card and

try to bank at least 20% of the total amount that you'll need every month. This way, you can be ready to publish in five months. If you need more time to complete your book, give yourself 10 months and put at least 10%-15% of the total amount that you'll need in your account every month. Do not pinch off this account unless it is absolutely necessary. Try not to put in less than what you've committed unless it is an absolute necessity. If by some unforeseen act, you have to put in less this month, try to add in double next month to make up for it.

4. Dedicate between 3-5 days a week to complete your book's goals. It will be

easier if you set a schedule and stick to it.

5. Go ahead and choose your tenacious ten
   if you can. They can be on your FB page
   or just random people that you have
   access to contact.

6. If you need a publishing company, start
   searching early and comparing the prices,
   reviews and packages. You can probably
   guess how many pages you will have
   when you're done. Always price the
   maximum amount of pages that you
   think your book will contain so that you
   can financially prepare yourself.

The purpose of this is to line everything and
everyone up for the completion of your project.
Seeing how much money you will need may

help you to be more patient with your writing and give you more time to learn the ins and outs of publishing a book.

Links to Help With Formatting

Formatting is or is not for you. Some people are just blessed with the patience and ability to learn fast, put something together and go over it again and again to make sure it's right. We call them meticulous. Then again, there are the average everyday Joes and Janes, and formatting may not be their forte. They wrote the book, but if they try to format the book, they may humiliate themselves as writers or publishers. Why write a book and then throw it in the trash? That's what you do when you try to do something that you are simply not patient or skilled enough to

25

do. You should know whether you are cut out for the job or not. Many times, authors that try to format their own books throw them together and publish them for the world to laugh at.

To write your book, you will need Microsoft Word or OpenOffice. Personally, I use OpenOffice. I downloaded it when I wanted to write an article and discovered that my new computer didn't have Microsoft Word. I have since become very comfortable and familiar with OpenOffice, and I prefer it over Word. You can use other writing programs, but most publishers will not accept documents that are not saved in Word format (.doc). OpenOffice does allow you to save books in several formats, including Microsoft Word.

Your book should contain:

•Cover

•Legal Notification and Disclaimer (This is a generation of lawsuit minded people, don't tempt them).

•Table of Contents

•Content, of course.

•Back Cover (If your book is only going to be published as an e-book, you don't need a back cover).

•ISBN Number

•Barcode (If you intend to print the book).

Optional pages include:

⟩   Acknowledgment Page

⟩   Preface

⟩   Prayer Page

You can also add in crediting, but this is not mandatory. An introduction is also needed to introduce the content of the book, and give the reader a preview of the content in the book.

When starting your book, leave one page open for the design. Personally, I like to have the design ready (if I know the name I will be using for the book). If I have it, I just upload it and begin the book.

After the cover design, you should add your credits page. On this page, you will list the people and companies that had a hand in publishing and distributing your book. In addition, you will list your book's 13 and 10 digit ISBN number.

After this, add your legal notification. This notification informs the readers not to plagiarize or illegally distribute your book. Next, you can proceed with an Acknowledgments page if you want one and then your Table of Contents.

(Golden Insert #1: Titles should trigger an emotional response. A good emotional response makes the reader want to buy your book. Let's do a boring Table and an intriguing one).

Book Title: A Guide For Waitresses: How To Get Tips 98% of the Time!

Review the table of contents below.

Boring	Intriguing
The Right Attitude	Am I Tip Worthy?
Will Get You a Tip	Characteristics of the
Some People Just	Non-Tipper
Don't Tip	Creative Ways to Turn a
How to Get a Tip	Tragedy Into a Tip
After Bad Service	

Some may say that they prefer the "boring" table of contents because they are straight to the point, but we are living in a generation that is emotionally driven. Straight to the point chapters often give off a lecture vibe, and people hate to be lectured, but they love to laugh. It is always good to incorporate your personality (and a few sillies) into the book to keep them interested. You can add some straight to the point chapters, but try to blend in some intriguing ones as well to encourage sells.

As you can see, in the 'Intriguing' column, I questioned the reader's work ethic. Your reader will often welcome this type of criticism because it is not written specifically to them, and at the same time; it helps them to understand that their problem may be a common issue amongst waiters and waitresses. People love to relate to others. In the TOC, I either tickled or challenged the reader. If the table of contents is funny, and the reader believes that he or she is going to learn and laugh at the same time, you have sparked their interest. But if your potential readers believe that your book is nothing more than learning material, ask yourself this: Who's going to use their tip money to download a Professor?

Another popular TOC is the how-to lines. How-to books have become quite popular since the unleashing of the live Internet. Before Google, we had to go to the library and conduct countless hours of research, but now all we have to do is conduct an Internet search for the subject and voila....we've got information. So, if your book is going to be informative, how-to headers are the way to go.

Great How-To Table Example:

How To Spot a Non-Tipper

How To Turn a Challenge Into a Tip

How To Relieve Stress On the Job

Content Text:

Make sure your text is one of the basic fonts:
Arial, Times New Roman, Helvetica, Tahoma,
Verdana or Georgia. Georgia isn't my favorite,
since the numbers drop down below the line. If
I am going to write a semi-fancy or fancy book,
I'll use a Times New Roman or Helvetica font;
but if it's a casual book, Arial, Tahoma or
Verdana seems more fitting. Avoid using
excessively fancy fonts or cursive fonts.

In your writing, remember to challenge the
reader and add a little bit of your personality to

the book. People love to laugh, and if you're able to talk about personal experiences and relate to the reader, you may have yourself a loyal reader. In addition, try not to be too witty. Sure, you have a personality that makes others smile, laugh, and want to hear more from you; but your personality can't be "seen" in a book. Readers will only read what you say, and wit can sometimes come off as arrogance or a corny attempt to get a laugh.

Try not to trigger negative emotions if your book's title or synopsis doesn't warn the reader beforehand. Some people don't like to buy books that are sad, and if you spring it on them, you may lose the reader and get quite a few negative reviews. If you were writing a book about the abuse you've experienced, you have no choice but to add sad stories, but at least your readers expect this. Just make sure to add a happy ending because readers have come to expect this and when they don't get it, they often rate the book as a bad read. If you're damaged, that will translate into your book and this can be emotionally draining to your readers. Your book may read well and touch on many issues that the reader has experienced, but when people buy your books, they are often looking for remedies and encouragement, not countless sad stories and gloom. Think of it like this: There are many people with issues who will buy your book. They are not purchasing your book to add your issues on top of theirs; they are purchasing your book in hopes of seeing a light at the end of their situations.

General Formatting

General formatting starts with the writer. Of course, you won't just open up a document and start typing endlessly unless you intend to hire someone else for formatting. You may want to leave a couple of pages open to add your cover design, table of contents, legal notification, acknowledgments, introduction and so on.

In addition, the writer usually separates the subjects by chapter, by placing each chapter's start on a new page. You wouldn't run the whole thing together. Whatever document you write in is the very same document that will have to be formatted. Editors tend to charge double or more for poorly put together documents because they require more time to format.

First, decide what you'd like at the beginning. Let's go the typical route:

- Skip one page for the cover design.
- Skip one page for the credits.
- Skip one page for the legal notification.
- Skip one page for the acknowledgments.
- Skip one page for the table of contents.
- Skip one page for the introduction.
- Skip one page for preface, if you are going to have one.

Now, let's begin on page six.

If you took my advice and you're just beginning to write, you should have your subjects already listed in the table of contents. Just let each subject line lead you to the next subject line. Don't worry; you'll be able to add or delete subjects as you write the book.

Adding Page Numbers

You want your book to automatically add the page numbers to each page. This looks professional and stops you from having to go page by page manually typing the numbers yourself. Microsoft Word and Open Office both have that feature.

Microsoft Word

http://office.microsoft.com/en-us/word-help/add-and-format-page-numbers-HP001226513.aspx

OpenOffice

http://wiki.services.openoffice.org/wiki/Docum
entation/OOoAuthors_User_Manual/Writer_G
uide/Page_numbering

Inserting Table of Contents

Microsoft Word

http://office.microsoft.com/en-us/word-
help/create-a-table-of-contents-or-update-a-
table-of-contents-HP001225372.aspx

OpenOffice

http://wiki.services.openoffice.org/wiki/Docum

entation/OOoAuthors_User_Manual/Getting_S

tarted/Creating_a_table_of_contents

Linking the Table of Content to the Chapters

This is what your e-book needs to give it

character and ease of use. Before linking,

however, be sure to make a copy of your book

that is not linked for print purposes.

Microsoft Word

http://office.microsoft.com/en-us/onenote-

help/create-hyperlinks-to-pages-sections-and-

notebooks-HA010209169.aspx

OpenOffice

http://ezebooktemplates.com/how-to-make-

your-table-of-contents-linked-in-openoffice-writer-solution-2

Adding Headers and Footers

Microsoft Word

http://office.microsoft.com/en-us/word-help/insert-headers-and-footers-HP001226486.aspx

OpenOffice

http://wiki.services.openoffice.org/wiki/Documentation/OOoAuthors_User_Manual/Writer_Guide/Creating_headers_and_footers

Formatting For Kindle

http://kindleformatting.com/formatting.php

Note: If you purchased the print version of

this book, please email me at

info@tiffanykameni.com, and I'll send the e-

book version to you so that you can access the

clickable links. You will need to show proof of

purchase, and I will have to verify your

purchase with the printer.

What's In a Name

Sometimes, we can be as corny as a cob.

The name of your book is very important. Most first-time authors believe that their books are so good that the name of the book isn't that important. How will someone know that your book is good if they never purchase it? Truthfully, some names are so ridiculous that they inspire best-sellers because they trigger the curiosity of potential readers. When the books are good, they begin to sell through word of mouth; but some names are so ridiculous that the writer only earns the right to call him or herself an author. Nevertheless, they don't earn a dollar in sells for their books.

A name doesn't require a lot of thought; it's the ones that think too hard that actually hurt the sell of their books. One of the most common errors I find with many first-time authors is that they are determined to name their book before they start to write it. Again, doing this places limitations on the author because it is common to end up branching out into different subjects as the book comes together. It is better to write the book and then come up with the name for it.

Another great folly is being anxious to publish the book. Oftentimes, authors will find themselves wanting to skip over editing, and any other service their books may need simply because they are eager to publish the books. I still have times where I want to hurry up and

put a book on the market, but I have learned to
not listen to those urges, take my time and
review the book thoroughly before publishing it.
Every time that I have prematurely released a
book, I have **always** ended up regretting it
because eventually I'll run into errors whenever
I read the book. This can be absolutely
humiliating, not to mention it can hurt the sells
of your books. And when that eagerness shows
up in our book's name, it does great damage to
the sells. Let me give you an example:
Patty wrote a book about relationships and how
to improve them. Her book is a great read, but
after finishing her book, Patty tries to come up
with a name for her new book. In her haste, she
has gone from wanting to find "the" perfect
name to just wanting to find "a" name for the

book. In the midnight hour, an idea comes in. She decides to call the book *Relationship Guidance Counselor: A How-To Guide to a Better Relationship*. Patty publishes her book, and is ready for some shut eye. What just happened here? Patty just assassinated her book with her eagerness. Her title gives off the impression that Patty is a guidance counselor. Before she continues, Patty had better utilize her disclaimer to let the readers know that she is not a counselor; she works at a local supermarket as a cashier. She has just put herself in the path of the lawsuit lady who may be looking for someone to blame for the failure of her marriage, and Patty's looking like a wide-open receiver. Next, what Patty did not consider is that her book will mostly sell to married people because singles rarely look for professional counseling. Singles often look for free ways to fix their relationships, and if that doesn't work, they look for a way out of the relationship. Married people know that it's not that simple because there are fees and legalities involved. Many married couples will look for outside professional help, whereas a single would just look for advice from a friend or two.

Let's say a married woman named Rebecca runs out and sees Patty's book. Rebecca's marriage is hanging by a string, so she thinks Patty's book may be what she needs to save her marriage. She purchases the book and reads it; all the while, her marriage is shattering before her eyes. There's a big problem here: Patty's book was written for singles. In her book Patty advises the readers to play psychological games with their lovers to get them into submission. Desperate and heartbroken, Rebecca administers the advice to her marriage, and all of a sudden; her husband moves out and sends her divorce papers. He wanted Rebecca to be upfront and truthful with him; he wanted her to put the emotions, games and manipulations away, but her last-ditch attempt to manipulate him just persuaded him that a divorce was inevitable. He verbalizes this to his soon-to-be ex-wife, and she's livid because Patty's book just helped her destroy what was left of her marriage.

You may be thinking that this is an unlikely

scenario, but you're wrong. People do buy books because of the impression the name gives them. All the same, people do write books to intentionally deceive people into buying their books; their sole focus is to sell the book, but they don't consider the lives that will be destroyed because of their advice. That's why lawyers are on standby. This is to say that you need to be careful with your book's name.

What should you call your book? How can you come up with a name that is inviting and attention grabbing? Your book's content should be covered in your book's name. In addition, the name has to trigger a reaction in the person's mind.

Try this approach:

1. Take about a week or two to come up with 10-20 names. List the ones you prefer the most starting from most preferred title to least preferred title.

2. Create a separate list of those names and type them randomly on a sheet of paper. Be sure to list your contact information on that paper (preferably email). Print between 20-40 copies of that paper. *(Be sure your book is print ready before you do this to deter name theft).*

3. Go to the mall or the location where your target audience frequents. Conduct a survey by stopping 20-40 <u>friendly</u> faces. Hand them the paper and ask them to choose the titles that they would be more

likely to purchase. Ask them to pick the five that they would prefer; listing them in the order in which they would prefer them. If they are in a hurry, ask them to take the paper home with them and email the answers to you. Let them know that you will send them a free copy of your new book (in e-book format) once it's published. *(Be sure to get their email addresses, ensuring them that you won't spam them).*

4. Tally up the results and use the names that the people like the most. Tallying is easy. Give ten points to each number one choice, seven points to the number two choice, five points to the number three choice, three points to number four

choice, and one point to number five

choice.

(Insert: Before printing the list, research and make sure that those names aren't already listed to an author).

Check out the example below:

Book Name	Total # 1 Votes	Total Tally
The Relationship Guidance Counselor	6	60
Love With No Limits	1	10
An Attitude Change- When A Relationship Breaks Down	5	50

Marry Me Or Else	5	50
The Ex-Terminator- Trying To Avoid Becoming An Ex	4	40
The Dog Ate My Relationship	2	20
How To Repair A Damaged Relationship	1	10
Breaking Up With The Idea Of Breaking Up	2	20
A Relationship With No Signal- Can You Hear Me Now?	3	30
The Relationship Mechanic	11	110

Your chart can be more elaborate, listing the total number of votes for each category, if you so choose.

5. Never use family members and friends because they will choose emotionally and not logically. For example, if you're a funny guy, and they know you to be that way, they'll find it hard to choose the serious and sensitive titles for you. They will choose titles that match your personality and not the content of the book.

6. Use subtitles if you can. Subtitles give more details about the book.

7. You can go the controversial route if you want to, but make sure that controversial title relates to the content of your book, or at least gives the reader an idea as to

Chapter 5- What's In a Name?

what the book is about.

How and Where to
Sell Your Books

I am a fellow Facebooker. I have sold many of my books by marketing them to my friends on Facebook. I have even gotten a couple of loved ones to buy the books, but that's not enough. Unless you want 15 sells and one review, you'd better heed this advice.

Some of your Facebook friends will buy to support you, but others don't want to buy your advice; they want it for free, and they'll pay for it with a "like." However many likes you get on a typical post, cut them in half and that's about how many sales you'll get on Facebook, if that.

Marketing online is the in thing, especially for e-books, but you should not entirely depend on online sales since the average Joe doesn't trust the Internet. He thinks you'll swipe his debit card information, drain him dry, and run off to Tahiti with your new-found fortune. Therefore, for print and e-books, you need to get out physically and market your books. As the word of your book spreads, you may find yourself getting more e-book sells than print sells.

For print books, you would need copies of your books to sign and sell. For e-books, you need flyers and a site to post your e-book for sale.

Here are a few places, on and offline, that you should try.

Online	Offline
www.amazon.com	Local malls and stores in and around your area.
www.books.google.com	Local bookstores in and around your area.
www.lulu.com	
www.tunesconnect.apple.com	Local libraries in and around your area *(if allowed)*.
www.barnesandnoble.com	(Hint: Anywhere people bring their wallets and purses. Stay away from

www.goodreads.com (For listing purposes) And of course, your own personal website	beaches, restaurants and recreational places where people go to relax. They may shoo you away because their purpose for coming to such a place was not to shop, but to relax. At a store or shopping center; however, people come ready to buy something).

Selling books. We all want our books to sell, but with so many authors coming on the scene, how do you make yours rise to the top to be noticed? It's simple: by being innovative with your content, design, branding, and marketing.

First off, competitiveness is a distraction. Never allow yourself to come under the pressure of a competitive mind because competitors have to spend too much time watching and trying to outwit their competition. They usually don't go too far from one another because the one that's behind is always trying to copy their competitor. Competition starts when two businesses level off, or are on the same level. Once they begin to compete, they are saying that they will remain at the same level and compete for business. For example, McDonald's and Burger King are competitors because they are on the same level. In some cities, McDonald's outshines Burger King, and in others, Burger King takes the crown. Wal-Mart and K-Mart are the same way. Therefore, if you find yourself competing with a person or a business, you are simply saying that you and that person are on the same level, or you are trying to get to their level. If you want to make it to the major leagues of marketing; however, you have to always strive to do better than the best. For example, let's say that Ulysses Jacob has written a book and sold 1,000,000 copies. His book touches on the same subject your book touches on. So, you desire to reach his height or outsell him. You can't do this by competing with him; you do this by checking out his protege, Cranston Crickler, who has sold 3,500,000 books. Now, develop a marketing plan to help you earn more sells than Mr. Crickler by at least 500,000. You don't do this by competing with Mr. Crickler, but by researching and implementing some of the same marketing tactics Mr. Crickler engaged in and by adding your own new and innovative marketing strategies. Your goal is to reach or exceed Mr. Crickler's height as far as sales. That way, when you reach Mr. Jacob's height, you'll still feel the need to grow, rather than level off and compete with Mr. Jacob. Always shoot higher than your mark.

For successful marketing, you also need: a press kit, video book trailer, professional photo, website and flyers.

Make sure you hire a professional to do your media. Branding is essential and will stand at the door of your success or failure. With branding, you NEVER go the cheap, do-it-yourself route unless you are professionally qualified to do so. One of the biggest tragedies to ever hit print media is poorly designed book covers with low-resolution images. If you want your book to sell to the masses, you need to have a design that will be accepted by the masses. If you refuse to invest in your project, what message are you conveying to your potential readers? The message that people will gather is that the content of the book is not worth their buck. If the book was so good, you'd invest in it; but because you knew it was a load of junk, you kept your money and hoped for theirs. I have literally seen people create a canvas, type the name of their book on it, and call it a cover just to save themselves a few hundred bucks. Nevertheless, they will openly proclaim that they are looking to sell more than a million copies of their books. How?

Yes, the process can be expensive, but there are ways to manage the costs.

Let's say the month is April and you want to publish by December. (We'll do a rough estimate for the cost of your branding).

Press kit. You can find someone that can design a professional PDF press kit for $50-$100. We'll just say it cost you $100.

Video infomercials can be expensive. You can be looking at about $500 for a professional infomercial, but you may be able to find someone to do one for as little as $50-$100 if you are willing to do the research. Be sure to review their portfolios!

Professional photo. This would depend on you and what you are looking for. If it's just a photo for the book, you could go in a local Wal-Mart and get the cheapest package, which usually runs anywhere from $7.95 (currently) to $14.95 for one pose.

If you're like me, you may want a whole session so that you can have multiple photos to choose from. In addition, you may want the extra photos for your upcoming website. Therefore, you would want to hire a professional photographer.

A good photographer can cost anywhere from $100-$500, depending on what you are looking for. Studio time is more expensive than outdoor photography. Studio shots are better because it allows the web designer to be more creative with your photos, but a good outdoor session will suffice. If you decide to go with an outdoor session, find an area that's scenic and is in close proximity to a hotel or a building where you can go in and do part of the session. You can call around to some hotels in your area. Sometimes, they will freely let you use their lobbies. There are even some hotels that you can just walk in and do the session because they are too big to know if you're a guest or an intruder. This goes especially for really big high-end hotels. People don't usually have time to question who you are, but a smaller hotel will take notice. As a photographer, I've done this a few times. I had my clients to meet me at large hotels on the beach and we walked in and did the sessions without ever being questioned or stopped. Talk with your photographer; he or she may know the perfect place. Be sure to bring a change of clothing, extra shoes, a towel to dry off and your makeup case (ladies). In addition, you can sometimes find free or inexpensive photographers on Craigslist trying to build their portfolios.

When finding a photographer online, be sure to meet in a public area. If they don't have a website, don't work with them. To ensure your safety, you should never meet a stranger in a secluded place. Always meet in the daylight hours in well-lit areas where there is a constant flow of foot traffic. For example, if the photographer suggests a secluded area on a beach after dawn, it is better to decline that offer unless you are taking plenty of people with you. It is always a great idea to bring extra people with you who won't be in the photos, but are just there for security and support. For the ladies, you should always have a man or a couple of men with you.

Be sure to check out the photographer's portfolio and their photo. When you arrive at the session, if the person in the photo is not the same photographer present, don't exit your car.

When searching Craiglist, click on the state and city nearest you. Next, look under the *Services* tab and select *Creative*. After clicking on *Creative*, try the following search terms:

- Free photographer
- Photographer building portfolio
- Portfolio photographer
- School photographer
- Cheap or inexpensive photographer

Don't always take the first person that you see because some photographers have old equipment and their photos don't come out so well. Compare their photos to the work of other photographers. In the end, you may discover that you have to go ahead and shell out the extra bucks, but it'll be worth it in the end. Before I got into photography, I searched Craigslist for a photographer. At first, I didn't know the difference between quality photos to below-average photos. As the days passed, I continued to go back and look at the portfolios and I began to see a difference in the clarity. My cheap side was screaming to go for one of the photographers that was in the limited budget that I'd created, but my heart was saying to go to the photographer who was obviously passionate about their work. To this day, I'm happy that I chose to ignore my cheap side and I went with the excellent photographer. That choice alone set in motion a chain reaction of excellence that continues to follow me to this day.

Another way to search for free photographers is to contact some local universities. Check to see if they have a photographer training program or classes for photography. If they do, their students need portfolios and will oftentimes do the work for free. Don't be ashamed to ask. The worst thing they can say to you is no.

Avoid camera phones and photographers with traditional digital cameras. While some of them may be good, they aren't the best of cameras. A nice DSLR camera will give you a high resolution shot. Now if you just can't afford this, go and buy a high megapixel digital (9 megapixels is good) camera for about $100, go outside around 5 or 6pm when the sun is going down and do a session. That way, you won't have too much sun in the photo. Also, you may need a few photos on a solid background for your graphic designer. You can go indoors and take a few in front of a white wall, but if you can find a solid space outside, that would be better because natural lighting is great for photos. Always take 100 or more photos so you can sort through your photos and possibly find a few that you love, rather than settling for what you like. This session should take about an hour or less. If you plan to go somewhere outside of walking distance from your residence, be sure to take a few test photos outdoors before you leave the house to make sure you like the way you look. This way, if you don't like your hair, makeup or outfit on camera, you can easily go and change it before the session. Either way, I strongly suggest that you hire a professional and not try to go out the cheap way because books that are designed and formatted professionally usually sell more copies.

Websites can be expensive. There are a lot of do-it-yourself routes, but I highly advise against them. If you search long and hard enough, you will find what you want for a reasonable price.

Your website's domain should either the book's name or the author's name followed by dot com. For example, my website is my name: Tiffany Kameni. (www.tiffanykameni.com)
I took this route after having published several books. It was too costly and too ineffective to try to market four websites to one person, so I

put all of my books under one roof: my name. Nevertheless, if you know your book is going to be the only book you publish or the only book you'll publish within the next couple of years, buying the domain for your book's title can be a good idea. In addition, there will be books that you consider hobby books, and others that you will consider major books. If you consider your book one of your major books, you can get a domain and site for it. One of my major selling books is called <u>Wise Her Still</u>, so I purchased the domain www.wiseherstill.com.

Be sure to avoid long domain names. One of my books is called *Christian and Married: How To Be One Without Losing the Other.* How silly would it be for me to buy

www.christianandmarriedhowtobeonewithoutlo

singtheother.com

Sadly enough, people REALLY do this. If I

wanted to buy a domain for this book, I

understand that I need to keep the domain

short. I could go with

www.christianandmarried.com or

www.candm.com. That wouldn't hurt my

search results, since the header of my site would

read, *Christian and Married: How To be One*

Without Losing the Other. My Google listing

will not be affected by my domain, but rather by

my metadata.

If you can get your name and it's not too long,

go for it. If your name is Mary Timmons, you

would just get www.marytimmons.com, but if

your name is Alessandra Karbashewsky, purchasing www.alessandrakarbashewsky.com isn't the best idea. You would want to go with something shorter like www.alessandra.com or www.alessandrak.com. You could even consider domains like www.alessk.com or www.alessandra.org.

A decent website should cost you anywhere between $200-$1000. Sometimes, you may even find a cheaper one, but it also depends on what you are going for and how dedicated you are to the search. If you want one for just the book, you could just get a squeeze page or simple website. Just a page or two should cost you about $99-$350. Nevertheless, if you purchase your personal name as a domain, you will need:

Home Page, About Page, Book Page (or Store), Contact Page. A simple site like this without the bells and whistles, should run you around $399 and up. You may be able to find someone to do it for about $200, but be sure to check out their portfolio. Don't hire someone just because they can do sites and you can afford their services. Having no site is better than having a poorly designed site.

Many people end up hurting their own image by hiring family members or friends to design their websites, or they give this project to anyone who volunteers to throw them something together. They do this because they don't want to shell out the money. As a result, they end up with awful websites consisting of several fonts, colors, and moving objects scrolling the screen. While on Facebook, the author *(we'll call him Steve)* notices other authors putting up the link to their sites and promoting their books. Steve's curiosity gets the best of him, and he begins to check out their sites and these author's sites are looking better than good! Steve goes back and clicks on his site with his eyes finally wide open and is suddenly conscious and ashamed about the mess that he's got spinning around on the Internet. Steve begins another search for another web designer that's going to cost him more money when he could have simply done this right the first time around.

Last, but not least, there are the flyers. A flyer designer can range from $50-$100, plus you have printing costs, so we'll just say $100-$150 for your flier budget.

Remember, it's April and you want to be published by December, so you now have to come up with $1,000 to $1,500 by December. This gives you 8 months to come up with the funds. That's roughly a little over a hundred, roughly up to $200 to save per month.

Now, this is just for marketing; that fee doesn't include the editor, publishing fees, printing costs, purchasing an ISBN, purchasing a barcode and whatever else you might need.

What if this is too much for you? I'll tell you how to get around a lot of it and save thousands in the next chapter.

It is better to plan ahead and you can learn to do much of the work yourself, but you have to learn to do it professionally. For example, you will need a write up about the book (synopsis) for the back of the book and an author's bio. You could do these yourself and have your friends and family to read over them, or if you know someone personally who is good with writing, enlist their services. As far as designing; however, **HIRE A PROFESSIONAL!!!**

A few more tips to consider:

1. Your family and friends will not help you get to the best-seller list. Sell them some books, but don't expect much.

2. If you have a secular job, take flyers to work and leave them in the lounge if

allowed.

3. Ask everyone you know if they'll help get you at least five sells.

4. Ask every buyer to come back and give you a review.

5. Avoid negative people. In addition, avoid politically correct people and individuals who like controversy. Especially power hungry souls. I know a few of these type and I would literally pay them **not** to buy my books. They'll only give you negative reviews, bad press and fruitless suggestions to puff themselves up and appear smart.

6. Set up a booth in a store and offer a reward to the 100th buyer or a drawing at about 5pm. Make sure the giveaway is

worth it. Nobody wants to win a pair of socks with your name on it. Take about $25 and put together a gift basket. *(Or pay a professional to put it together).* To be eligible, they must buy a book. Now, this is if you want sells, but it is better to get people that will actually read the book.

Pricing Your Book

Oh, the great dilemma. You're finished, but what should you charge? You go around looking at books with similar subjects and that competitive feeling tries to sneak back up on you. For example, your book is about building computer programs. You find about 35 more books on Amazon that have the same subject matter, and they range in price from .99 to $49.99. What's the difference? Why is this guy's book so inexpensive and the other guy's book so expensive? The answer is: content, popularity, aim and sometimes lack of knowledge. Mr. $49.99 may have conducted months or years of research and is compiling his own findings, and his book may be selling to universities or a particular major in the universities may require each student to have this book. Because it's mandatory, he can charge $49.99. Then again, he could be a greedy unknown author who thinks that people are going to pay him fifty bucks to teach them how to do the same thing that another author is teaching for $4.99.

Mr. 99 Cents; however, may have summarized several books that he read on the subject and simply gave his opinion. While his book is inexpensive, don't write him off just yet. The difference between the two prices can be a wide opened gap, but the amount netted by the two may be the same. If the expensive book is being purchased by college students, at the rate of

1,000 sales a year, that would mean that the total yearly earnings for the seller is $49,990. Sounds like a lot, right? It's an okay amount, but you should always shoot for more. What if the 99 cent book sells more than 500,000 copies in a year? That seller just bought in a whopping $495, 000! Why did his book sell so many copies? Because it was within reach for almost everyone, and he marketed to more than just universities. In addition, more than 200,000 of those sales probably came from college students looking to get a helping hand or a better understanding.

Therefore, how much you sell it for should depend on:

- Real Demand

- Target Audience

- You

Real Demand

Who is going to need your book? Will it be used by universities, businesses or some government agencies as a learning tool? If your answer is no, let's keep the price low.

Is your book needed in today's market?

Are you offering knowledge that hasn't been published before? If so, this ups the demand for the book.

Have you paid a professional editor to clean up the book? If your answer is yes, you can ask for more. If your answer is no, let's keep the price low.

What about cover design and formatting? Is it

professionally done or is it just done?

How many pages are in the book?

Here is a chart that I drafted below. Please understand that this chart is drafted on my opinion only and should not be used as a blueprint for pricing.

Page Number	Pro Editor	Pro Setup	E-book	Print
10 through 25	No	No	0.99	3.99 or less
26 through 45	No	No	1.99-3.99	5.99 or less
46 through	No	No	3.99-4.99	7.99 or less

65				
65 through 100	No	No	4.99- 5.99	9.99 or less
100 through 150	No	No	5.99- 6.99	9.99- 11.99

For every professional service you have, add one dollar more to the above posted pricing. For example, if you have a 24 page booklet that has not been professionally edited, but does have a professional setup (formatting, book cover), then you'd go up from a .99 e-book to $2.99 for the e-book, but you'd have to drop a dollar because you didn't hire a professional editor, so your book may be flawed. You'd sell your book for $1.99.

E-book pricing is very flexible, but you should always keep it low, especially for your first book because you want to get the world familiar with you and create a demand for your books. Don't have dreams of grandeur and billions of dollars falling out of the sky just yet. $4.99 is reasonable, but having an e-book for $4.99 means that you have to have a print book for at least $9.99. My recommendation, for your first e-book is .99 to $4.99. This book is your introduction. You can also give the book away on Amazon for 24 hours freely just to get book reviews. This would increase your ranking on Amazon and possibly get you listed on their best-sellers list.

Printing, on the other hand, depends on how

many print copies you order. The more books you order upfront, the less printers charge you per unit. For example, I ordered 100 copies of one of my books that was about 79 pages long, and the printing company charged me $311 plus shipping. Therefore, I paid $2.88 per book. I turned around and sold those books for $7.99. My asking price was $9.99, but I settled for $7.99 as a part of my marketing strategy. With 100 units of my book, I brought in $799. This enabled me to go back and reorder 100 copies at $311, thus allowing me to keep or net $488. I then invested $200 of what I netted back into marketing. Why is that? I understand that you want to keep everything you net, but your goal is not to sell a thousand copies and run to Hawaii. With your first book, your goal is to promote yourself as an author. You are setting up the market for your second book, believe it or not. You want to get your name known as a best-selling author; not just try to make a few hundred bucks and retire. Once your book has become a best-seller or has sold more than a thousand copies, you should be working on or have completed your second book. When people find that they enjoyed your first book, they'll tell others about it, and they'll look for other books written by you. The people that they tell will just be coming in, purchasing your first book and this cycle continues. While you may not sell ten units a week initially, if you market, plan and promote the right way; you are creating highways of income that are simply under renovation. Once they open up, you will need an accountant to help you direct the traffic.

For printing, always set your price where you'll make a 50% profit, in addition to shipping costs. If you can find a local printer, check them out. Look at the quality of their books, compare their prices to online printing companies and other local printing companies and decide if they are a better fit for you. Sometimes they cost more than online printing companies, but you have to factor in that you are saving on would be shipping costs. Plus, with a lot of online printing companies, there are a lot of hidden and surprise costs that may catch you off guard. They usually don't run anymore than $100, but hidden fees cut into your budget. The online printing company that I first used made me shell out an additional $35, citing I had to send them a new cover because the cover I'd designed originally did not fit their guidelines. Even though they didn't print it or do anything with it, they knew they could charge more, and they did. So, with online companies, it is always good to put up another $100-$200 just in case they ask for more. With local printers, you can take your files in and get everything approved before you pay anything.

Cutting Out the Middle Man

I am not a fan of paying extra people to do work that I can do on my own; therefore, I had to learn patience and the skills I needed to get around the men and women in the middle. Now, one of the middle men that you can't get around is the editor. No matter how good you are with spelling, punctuation and grammar; you will more than likely make some grammatical errors in your book. Even as a stellar speller, you will often overlook your own errors because you are familiar with how you talk and write. Oftentimes, the author doesn't see their errors until they have published their books, and they open them to read them objectively.

Formatting is good, but you can do it yourself, if you have the patience and the skill. Now, if you are not a patient person, don't do the formatting because you'll get frustrated midways through and throw the rest together. You can learn to format and link your chapters together online. It does take time and plenty of patience. You will need to be Microsoft Word or OpenOffice savvy; otherwise, everything you read in relation to formatting will be foreign to you. *(Please note that if you are hiring a publisher, they will likely format the book for you. Do not attempt to format it yourself or your publisher will either charge you more money or send it back to you to be corrected).*

Again, if you don't have money for an editor, check your friends and family. You may have someone that is really good with spelling, punctuation and grammar. Now, using them is a desperate reach, considering that they are not a professional, but letting a few people read over it and correct it won't hurt you. Be sure they are people that you trust. Put it in the wrong hands and you might find that Cousin Sue has published your book as her own. This is rare, but just be careful.

(Golden Insert: Copyright is just $35 when done online and you are protected immediately, even while your application is in

processing. Therefore, if Cousin Sue steals it, you can take the necessary legal steps and sue Sue).

Can't afford a website right now? Go with a blog. Blogs are now the in thing, and are quickly replacing websites. Two of my favorite blog sites are www.blogger.com and www.wordpress.com. You can design the blog and attach your domain name to it.

When designing the blog, please follow these rules:

1. Don't be extremely colorful. Colors are pretty, but you don't need 12 of them. Three colors are usually my limit. *(By the way, I'm also a professional web*

designer).

2. Use one font for the body text and one font for the heading text.

3. Create multiple pages for your blog and place the book cover and info about the book on the first page. You should also create an author's page and a contact page. Make sure the reader can purchase the book from the site. Paypal is my number one choice. Google Checkout is good too, but I've been using Paypal for years, so I'm a little more partial to them.

4. Upload only professional photos of yourself. Don't cheapen up your site with photos of you that are blurry and non professional just because you look cute on the photo.

5. Let that blog be for your book and your book only, unless it is a personal site for yourself. Since Blogger and Wordpress are free, you can create multiple sites and attach domains to them. If the site is for you (ex: www.yourname.com), you could place your photo on the front page and info about the new book and everything else you do.

6. When writing your bio, speak in either second person or first person, but never both. It should not read, for example: Mark Macy is a man of many words. With his new book, he has uncovered the truth behind illegal adoptions and is bringing it to you firsthand. I really enjoyed writing this book. It gave me an

opportunity to share with you, the reader,

my experiences with illegal adoptions

and the impact it has on; not just the

families involved, but the children.

It is always better to speak in second person and

better to let someone else write it, but if you want

to do it yourself, just remember: let someone read

over it.

7. Sell yourself first, and then the book.

Buy your own domain name. I have found that

many people are clueless about domains. They

will pay someone a monthly fee for a domain

when they could easily go to www.godaddy.com

and get one for around $7.99- $12.99. Also

check out some coupon sites to see if there are

any discount codes that you can use to get the

domain for cheaper. One great site for coupons is www.retailmenot.com. (Note: RetailMeNot is no longer a favorite because each retailer's page is now littered with other ads; therefore, I recommend you do a Google search.

Your Target Audience

Before you can begin to target market, you must know who your target audience is. If I am writing a cookbook for dieters, it wouldn't be wise for me to market it to an obese man holding a foot-long hotdog and a Slurpee. Sure, he may be the one that needs it the most, but he has to make that decision on his own. The best route is to go to health food stores, popular tracks in your town, the gyms in your area or anywhere health conscious people are.

You need to find your own market. Ask yourself:

- In what age group are the people that will

more than likely find my book
irresistible?

- What income bracket will find my book
  more appealing? If you're talking about
  buying property, you have to market to
  people who can afford to buy it, unless
  you're teaching individuals how to buy it
  with little to no money down and
  affordable monthly costs.

- What ethnic group is more likely to buy
  my book?

- What are the general hobbies of
  individuals who are most likely to buy
  my book?

- Where do the people that fit my criteria
  frequent?

Locating your market can make the difference between a no-seller and a best-seller. It is very common for a first-time author to try to market to the whole wide world. If you have written a recipe book for people with diabetes, would you go to a college campus to promote it? Determining your target is relatively easy. If I am writing a book about relationships, I know that my market would be in the age range of 18-30, but if I am writing about marriage, my market would be in the age range of 25-50, so I'd stay away from universities and concentrate on stores where individuals around 25 and older frequent. On a typical weekend, the mall is full of teenagers, so it may be a great place if you're trying to market to the younger genre.

What about technical fields; for example, computers? Your market would not span beyond 40 years old. While you may find some 40 plus year-old techs, you'd find more of your target market in the 18-30 crowd. I would also target university heads, as it may be a great teaching tool.

For a recipe book, my target audience would be somewhere between 25 years of age to 60 years of age, and they'd more than likely be blue collar families. Because the less a person makes, the more inflexible they are when buying new foods.

For fiction and adventure books, your audience would probably be 18-25 years of age. You shouldn't try to market a book about a talking karate bear with a Mohawk on a mission to rescue his cubs to 50 year old men.

Marketing Your Book

Now that I have determined who my target audience is, I need to market my book to them; but how?

Here are a few tips:

1. Book signings. Call around and see if some of the malls, local stores, churches and so on would let you set up a table and do a book signing. Choose the day of the week that is the busiest.

2. Get online. Online isn't your major market, but it is a market. Facebook is a great marketing tool, but you will have to befriend (add) and promote your book to your target audience.

3. Flyers are helpful campaign tools. If you walk around the mall handing out flyers to everyone, more than 50% of the recipients are going to trash your flyers. Those flyers were costly to you, so be sure to give flyers only to your target audience or the people who seem interested in obtaining a flyer. Here's a great idea: Purchase a box of envelopes and some <u>admit one</u> tickets. You can find them at Wal-Mart, Office Depot and other stores that sell stationary. In each envelope, place a flier and a ticket, and be sure to keep the other part of the ticket. Each ticket has a duplicate. Let the people know that you are promoting your new book and will be giving away

$100 to one of the buyers. Now, this may seem scary to you, considering you may not earn $100 that day, but the drawing doesn't have to be set for that day. Set the drawing up to take place two weeks from that day. Tell each person that every time one of their friends buys a book, they will get another entry. Get out there and don't stop selling until you have earned that $100. I know you don't want to give away your earnings, but remember, right now you are just trying to get your book into the hands of new readers and get your name out there. Be sure to only market to those that fit your target audience, and be sure to not be out on the day of the drawing because out of 50 people, you will only have one winner. Needless to say, some people don't take losing well and may request a refund. Just give them the site or blog where they'll be able to go and see who won.

4. Dress to impress. You need to look like a SUCCESSFUL published author, not just another desperate man or woman who wrote a book. Try not to go overboard. A big flower in your hair won't invite people over. Try looking professional and inviting, or try looking like your target audience. If you're writing a book about something casual like haircuts for the modern man, you could come out casual considering your book has a casual undertone.

5. Be polite...even to the rude people.
    Sometimes rude people do come back
    and buy the book, and even if they don't,
    you don't want to engage in a
    confrontation with them.

6. Avoid parking lot sales. You'll scare your
    would-be customers.

7. Research the Internet for every place you
    can list your book.

8. Another reward you can offer...if you
    know someone with a good video camera
    (*preferably a professional videographer*) is
    a chance to be in your book trailer. Tell
    them that you are looking for five people
    to feature in your commercial, and if they
    buy your book and leave a review on
    Amazon, they will be entered in for the

chance to be in this trailer. Give them a specific date and time when the winners will be announced. This will help you in several ways. First, using real people for interviews will bolster your sells. Secondly, those very same people are going to promote you when they are promoting the fact that they were in your commercial. Lastly, getting one-on-one contact with people will help you to become more confident when promoting your book. *(Please don't use your cellphone video or a digital camera. You want the commercial to be professional).*

9. Place your flyers in barber shops and hair salons.

10. Buy t-shirts and give them away as

promotions. There is nothing better than walking advertisements.

11. Contact a few radio stations and ask if they will conduct an interview with you. Local blog radios are great tools because you can embed the audio of the show on your website. Don't worry about the number of people visiting their show; look at it as an opportunity to promote your book.

12. Go to your local Chamber of Commerce and get a list of events coming up in that year. Try to be at every one of those events with your books. See what permissions you have to get first.

13. Give away free copies of your book. Create events, for example, in public

places such as the beach or the park.

Bring a camera, a few helpers and a

xylophone. Be sure to film the event,

giving away t-shirts and copies of your

book. Post those videos on your website.

These events are crowd grabbers because

people like to be filmed and people are

attracted to free stuff. For those that

didn't win, offer them the opportunity to

buy your book and get a free t-shirt with

the purchase.

14. Ask people to create videos about your

book. If you approve them, they'll be

posted on your site.

15. Photo op. Create a huge billboard of

your book. A lot of stationary stores

could help you with this. Have them cut

a large hole in the billboard, ensuring that the hole is large enough for a large head to go through and come out with ease. Go to the beach and invite people to take a photo with the billboard, or you can have them take photos with you or holding your book. They could even hold a sign with the name of your book on it. Next, post it to your site and be sure to give them a copy of the photo. You could collect their email addresses or tell them the photos will be listed on your site for download. Be sure they sign a contract giving you permission to use the photos of them at will.

16. Another photo op. I have a book that is being printed and is on it's way to me.

Once it gets here, one of the things that I am going to do is go out and try to kill two birds with one stone. I need to build my photography portfolio. Plus, I want to sell those books. Therefore, I'll be offering a free photo shoot (about 20 minutes) to all the people who purchase my book and leave me a review on my book. The photo shoot will take place 2-3 weeks from the day of my signing. You may say, "Hey, this is coercing people to buy your books! That's not fair!" The strategy isn't supposed to be fair; however, I will be marketing to my target audience. You'll understand when you read the next chapter: *The Tenacious Ten.* Anyhow, I will go to a public park on a designated day (with my husband) at a designated time. Every purchaser will come there and show off the ticket that I gave them and get their session at the time we agreed upon. While you may not be a photographer, I am sure that there are PLENTY of photographers in your area that want to and need to build their portfolios. Find them and see if they'd be willing to do a photo session of about 15-20 people. Your goal, that day is to make back what you put into getting that book. I don't have to give away CDs or prints, I will just tell the clients to bring their computers and I will transfer the photos onto their computer. Simple enough and everybody wins.

17. Get plenty of business cards. You can go to a local stationary store, but as for me, I usually go through www.vista.com. Hand them out to your target audience.

18. Call the major store headquarters to see if they'd be willing to list your book. Be aware that most major retailers will not list self-published books because many self published authors bypass professionalism just to save a buck. They will often make exceptions when you present a quality product to them, so be sure to hire professionals if you want your books to sell in major retail stores.

19. Contact bloggers to see if they'd write a blog about your book. Send them a free e-copy.

20. Who can resist a cute three to five-year-old? Enlist their help, only if your book is child friendly. Create a brochure and talk to some local schools and see if they are willing to allow the children to sell your books for rewards to their family and friends. Create a reward pamphlet detailing what each student will get for selling in each number bracket. For example, one to two books, they'll get a small box of candy; something inexpensive, but rewarding. *(You could get this from the dollar store).* Three to five books could get them a teddy bear and a box of candy. 40-50 books would get them a bicycle. Calculate how much of a profit you will have made and deduct

a small amount of that to buy the gifts. So, if I paid $311 for 100 books and I profited about $488 on the book, I could use 50% of that $488 to buy gifts. Again, I must reiterate that your goal is to get your name out there not to turn a profit just yet.

21. Take the Internet by storm. Whatever the name of your book is, place it everywhere, including in your signature. Ask your friends and family to create blogs about the book. Create a Facebook, Twitter, Myspace or Bebo account just for your book. The more you come up in Google, the better.

22. Participate in author workshops.

23. Trade links with others. *(Website links,*

that is).

24. Give an audio presentation (about 30 seconds) about your book and place it on your site and anywhere audio can be uploaded.

25. (For Self Help Guides) Print copies of your book and send them to about 20-100 local prisoners. While this may seem like a horrible marketing strategy, it gets the books real reads. Remember, those prisoners do often have family members on the outside that they will happily promote your book to. Not to mention, the lives that could be changed through the availed knowledge.

26. Offer coupons. Sure, you want $9.99 for your book and you refuse to accept

anything less. Try this strategy: Market your book at $11.99 and offer a $2.00 coupon on sites like www.retailmenot.com. Or if you'd be willing to accept $7.99 for it, offer a $4 coupon. Did you know that there are people out there that are addicted to sales? They don't buy things because they need them; they buy them because they are on sale! While they may not make for real readers; oftentimes, people like this give away their purchases as gifts to people who they know love to read.

27. Travel and market. Don't just market locally. Get out of the city, state or country.

The Tenacious Ten

Who are the tenacious ten and how can they help me with my book?

Let's say you've completed and published your book. You've gotten it on Amazon, to name a few and now you're waiting for buys. You research books that are like yours and they've gotten quite a few sells and comments, and then there are those that seem to be just sitting there.

Of course, you want your books to sell and be read. Let's say; for example, you have a Facebook fan page, and you've gotten 12 likes and next week; the number has graduated to a whopping 13 likes. What's the problem? People don't flock to low numbers. People like to be a part of something big; therefore, in order to amp up the likes, you would have to go to people personally and ask them to like your new page. You'd probably even have to offer coupons, contests, and giveaways just to motivate people to like your page. Once you have gotten about 500 likes, you will find that your page grows at an alarming speed.

The same way of thinking goes on in the book world. For example, if your book is on Amazon and it does not have any ratings, most people will pass it by because they don't want to be the first to review your book. They want to hear from others that your book is worth their time.

They may go on to buy a book that is less informative and more expensive because that person has quite a few comments and likes. How do we remedy this? You should always seek to get at least ten comments on Amazon as soon as possible, because the more comments your book has, the more people will believe that it's worth buying. How do you get ten comments so fast? Give away 20 copies of your book in e-book format. Make it clear to them that you are giving away the book in exchange for their testimony. Ask them to read the book and go to Amazon to leave their reviews. Out of those 20, only 50% will comply. The other ten will keep saying, "I haven't read it yet" or "It just won't let me comment." The ten that do leave you a comment are your tenacious ten. They are the ones that are going to get the ball rolling on your book.

Do yourself this favor and avoid politically correct people, relatives, angry people, anxious people, impatient people and jealous people. Chances are, they won't leave you positive feedback. They'll grade you two stars and attempt to correct you publicly, and you can't really get mad at them for doing so. After all, you asked them to leave a you a review and they did. You just assumed they would know that you meant a **positive** review.

Be sure to get some reviews on your website and other sites that your book is posted on as well. Always seek to get reviews on the websites that get the most traffic.

Remember: One bad review can do more damage than five good ones.

The Poor Man's Way

Okay, we have went over a few ways that you can publish and sell your books for cheap. But, let's just say you are poor and just can't even afford to do it the cheap way. You need free. Now some of this advice I am about to give you is unconventional. They don't tell you how to do these things in normal books, because they expect you to at least have enough money to be called cheap.

Editor	Got an old English teacher, right? Did she at least like you? Do you know someone that is an English teacher, or is just good in English? Send them a copy of your book and ask them to edit it as a favor. In return, help them to launch a rewarding career in editing. If you don't at least know someone that has credentials, find about three people (or more) that you know are pretty good in English. Ask them all to read over and edit your book, but not at the same time. Give it to Cousin Sherry's

	daughter and once she's done with it, give it to the next one and the next one. What one doesn't catch, the other should.
Book Cover	Call or visit some of the local universities and see if they have any students in the graphics field who need something to add to their portfolio. You'd be amazed how many students would jump at the opportunity. In addition, go to www.craigslist.org and advertise the opportunity. In exchange, publish their name as the graphic designer in the book and let them use it in their

	portfolio. You can also use www.lulu.com to create a book cover.
Website	Call the local universities again to see if they have any students in the graphic's field who wants to add to their portfolios, or you can build your own website using tools like Weebly, Wix or Tripod.
Photography	A lot of colleges are packed with photographers who need models to align their portfolios. You just have to call around. In addition, I have helped many find inexpensive and sometimes free photographers on

	www.craigslist.org. If you don't see one on the site, advertise on the site in your search for one. Be sure not to meet in a secluded place. Be safe and always bring friends.
ISBN/ Barcodes	Can't afford one? Use www.lulu.com and/or www.createspace.com to publish your book and get a free one.
Book Formatting	Do it yourself. If you aren't that patient, find someone who is and give them something in exchange for their work. The younger crowd (12-25) is packed with young techs who could easily format your book

	without a sweat.
Copyright	Fork up the $35. A poor man's copyright is a simple email to yourself with your files attached, but if you're too poor or cheap to fork up $35, who are you kidding when you say you'll dish out a few thousand bucks for an attorney? If you don't pay for anything else, pay for your copyright. Go to www.copyright.gov and get your book registered before it leaves your hands.
Website	Get a blog and link a domain to it. www.blogger.com and www.wordpress.com are great

	tools.
Flyers	Flyers are usually $50-$99; however, if you can't afford to have one designed, try googling "Free Flyer Makers Online" or "Make a Flyer Online Free." You can print the flyer from home, but there's no getting around the ink and paper. It is; however, cheaper to go to a store like Office Depot and have some prints made, since ink cartridges and gas prices go hand-in-hand.
Press Kit	The same way you made this book, you can make a press kit. It's simple. Add your book cover as the first page, add a

	write up about your book on one page, a bio about yourself on the next page, an excerpt from the book and a contact page. Make a linkable table of contents and voila; you have a press kit!
Advertising	You need ads! Videos! Audio commercials! Okay, here's how you get this all done. Talk to 20 people (friends, family, strangers) and ask them to go and create an advertisement for your book on the site of their choice and send you the link. Or even better, have them to create a blog and market it.

Your goal is to dominate the search engines.

Use Windows Movie Maker to create an infomercial, if you don't know someone who can do it for you. If you don't have Windows, simply use Google and search the terms: *Create Commercial Online Free.* Then again...you can do it the same way you did the photography, call around the schools and ask about videographers.

Audio commercials are easy to come by. Go to www.blogtalkradio.com and start your own radio show. It's free! Talk about your book,

invite guests, or search out the

site to find anyone who will be

willing to do an interview with

you on their audio blogs. You

can also buy a DVR (digital

voice recorder) and record

yourself talking about your

book. DVRs are usually $25 and

up.

Search Google for the term:

advertise free, and sign up and

advertise on every site that will

let you.

Go to www.examiner.com and

find the Examiner in your area

and ask them if they'd be willing

	to write an article about you or your book. Frequent online message boards that relate to your book's subject and substance.

Other Helpful Links

Creating and Linking a Table of Contents in OpenOffice

http://ezebooktemplates.com

Start Numbering From Page 2 or Higher in OpenOffice

http://openoffice.blogs.com

Download OpenOffice

http://www.openoffice.org/download/

Learn OpenOffice

http://www.learnopenoffice.org/tutorials.htm

Microsoft Word (2007) Training

http://office.microsoft.com